Undefeat

MW00932749

Mental strength and peak performance.

Table of Contents

Introduction 3

Chapter 1:What Exactly is An undefeated mind? 6

Chapter 2: Develop Emotional Stability 11

Chapter 3: Positive Thinking is the Key................................ 15

Chapter 4:Build Self-Confidence...18

Chapter 5: Learn To Delay Gratification............................. 21

Chapter 6: Be Courageous 24

Chapter 7: Bounce Back When Life Knocks You Down 27

Chapter 8: Embrace Challenges 31

Chapter 9: Develop Flexibility...34

Chapter 10: Manage Stress Effectively.................................37

Chapter 11: Practice Greater Self-Awareness...................... 40

Conclusion..44

Introduction

What is an undefeated mind?

An undefeated mind entails partaking in the psychosomatic edge that permits one to accomplish extreme effort and efficiency despite the strains placed upon them by their competition, training, interactions, and internal dialogues. Specifically, when the strains are extreme or the situations become dire. At any time, the demands are the greatest when the features of an undefeated mind are the most obvious.

Three secrets in developing an undefeated mind were recently revealed by a former Navy SEAL and Navy SEAL instructor, Phil Black. These closely guarded secrets will lead you to the great levels of an undefeated mind and help you dominate your game and workout. They are easy to practice while also being highly effective and are used by some of the most elite athletes on this planet.

There are many aspects of an undefeated mind and mental training, but the principles are simple and can be rooted down to a few main components. It doesn't matter if it's for sports like baseball, basketball, tennis or boxing or for other fitness activities like running, weight lifting, or martial arts. These principles of mental fitness, the psychology of it, can be applied in any area.

First, what is an undefeated mind? An undefeated mind is the ability to persist when things go wrong, get difficult and/or become strenuous. It is the ability to keep your internal dialogue (your self-talk) positive despite the negative external occurrences.

From when you were born until the age of 18, you were told "no" about a 150,000 times. That is 700 times a month, or 22 times a day! People told you, "No, get away from there" and "Stop doing that". Some of these were to protect you from danger, some to prevent you from growing because of other people's fears or ignorance.

This caused you to become highly susceptible to negative influence. Psychologists have found that 77% of internal self-talk is negative and counteracting. Now do you realize how much of our potential is being held back?

I know you have likely heard that there are no limits on what we can be, have and do. This statistic pretty clearly shows that we are the ones that hold ourselves back more than anything else does!

Therefore, you must control your mind or "they" will do it for you. This is how the Navy SEALs do it:

Monitor your self-talk, that internal dialogue you have with yourself every day. Become a watcher of your mind. Do you have positive thoughts or negative ones? What do you feel like on a day-to-day and moment-to-moment basis? Are you adding to the negative side or the positive side? For two days, write down everything that is negative. Just your negative thoughts, you want to become aware of how much of what you think is negative. Remember, psychologists found that, on average, 77% or your internal talk is negative. What percent is yours?

Filter out negative events and thoughts. What kind of material do you read? What type of people do you hang out with? How often do you laugh with those around you? That is an indicator of how well things are going. Become purposeful about what you let into your mind, put on a filter and screen out any negative influence. Your environment, the people you associate with, and the things you read or listen to are big influences on the way you think. In a positive environment, it is much easier to weather through any storm that comes.

Reframe all the negative events in a positive light. Use your sense of humor and your brain will encode it differently. Just because something is negative doesn't mean you have to accept it as such. Much of life is how you respond to it. If your training is difficult and demanding, you could say, "Ha! Ha! This workout is killing me, is this all there is to it? I want some more, I'm just warming up. I'm tougher than all of this, you can't defeat me!"

Chapter 1:What Exactly is An undefeated mind?

Though an undefeated mind was initially used as a term to mentally prepare an individual and make them into a more formidable athlete, today it is used in a broader sense for goal achievement in multiple spheres of life. It refers to training people with a set of positive attributes to mentally equip them for handling challenging situations. In other words, an undefeated mind is about grit. The concept is widely used by sports psychologists, life coaches, corporate trainers and business leaders all over the world.

United States based researchers, Declan Connaughton, Graham Jones and Sheldon Hanton conducted extensive interviews with top level athletes, elite coaches and sports training psychologists to arrive at a definition of an undefeated mind - "having the natural or developed psychological edge that enables you to generally cope better than your opponents with the many demands (competition, training, lifestyle) that sports place on a performer; specifically, you must be more consistent and better than your opponent in remaining determined, focused, confident and in control under pressure."

Thus you can see that, though the definition is primarily sports-training centric, it can be applied to any life area to overcome challenging situations in your single-minded pursuit of a goal. The definition broadly translates into an undefeated mind being a sort of a "protective mental gear" that safeguards you in the face of increasing adversity. It equips you to sustain your determination, persistence and focus despite an onslaught of challenges. Obviously, circumstances in our lives don't always go as planned. Life often throws us off track with its myriad obstacles.

An undefeated mind is the tenacity to rise above these stumbling blocks. It is to take one devastating blow after another, yet emerge victorious. An undefeated mind is about developing resilience, strength and fortitude to manage your emotions when stuck in overwhelming situations. Essentially, it is about keeping yourself mentally strong, and listening intently to the voice within you that insists that you keep pushing, despite the prevailing trials. An undefeated mind creates a symbolic helmet over your head which braces you against elements that can mentally knock you off your game.

An undefeated mind is what sets apart a superstar from an average performer. It separates party gig performers from the crowd-pulling rock stars. A naturally gifted individual without an undefeated mind may end up achieving far less than a person with average ability, but which possesses an undefeated mind. As much as our ability is responsible for determining our success in life, the attitude that accompanies our natural abilities can have a huge effect on our overall wellbeing. An undefeated mind is an aggregation of self-motivation, emotional restraint, self- control, positive attitude, composure under fire, absolute energy and a "ready to go" mindset.

Consistency is the key to incorporating these traits into everyday life to reach new heights of success in multiple endeavors, from sports to music to computer programming to writing a book or finishing a dissertation. An individual with an undefeated mind takes challenges head on and even thrives in overcoming them. He/she displays a keen combination of skills, effort, resilience and positivity.

We often look at people who seem to be happy all the time in admiration and wonder if their life is free of adversities. We live under the delusion that such people are never faced with any challenges and seem to have a smooth ride in life. However, these "eternally happy" folks have a single trait that separates them from the others. They aren't free of challenging situations, far from it. They just possess a keen knack for dealing with these circumstances in a remarkably resilient way by being mentally tough. Tough situations don't seem to affect them much or discourage them from their goals. They keep going and show no signs of surrendering. Mentally tough people have a firm grip over their emotions and are seldom reactive to the things that would intimidate other people.

When it comes to sports or any other life goals, an undefeated mind is about being internally motivated. It is about creating inexhaustible reserves of mental strength and motivation to tap into when the going gets tough and there seems to be no way through. The force of your determination is influenced by how intensely you want to achieve something. While others play complacent, you can dramatically increase your chances of gaining an edge over them by sharpening your mental strength saw.

Life throws many unexpected challenges in our direction. What happens when the company you were employed with for the last 15 years suddenly closes up shop due to a global recession? Your entire world just turned topsy-turvy due to a situation that was beyond your control. What do you do next after finding yourself in a seemingly fearful situation? Should you simply dump your career? Take up the first job you find? Get back to learning and training yourself for better opportunities? Move into a smaller space to save rent? Many folks don't have it in them to rise up and get things going again. They will do everything, from blaming the unfortunate situation for being low on luck to acting helpless. You may have to compel yourself to get going. Why is it so tough? And how do you overcome your inability to act in tough situations? An undefeated mind training is all about this and much more.

An undefeated mind arms you with the ability to cope with the magnitude of fear, and to just go about doing whatever you are required to do and achieve your goals. It is courage, awareness and a proactive approach. There are a multitude of cognitive behavior therapies that train people to be more mindful of their goals and enhance their capacity to single-mindedly pursue them. An undefeated mind can perform in the best interest of your objectives despite an avalanche of distractions, obstacles and discomforts.

Setting intentions, channeling effort in the right direction and building up huge courage reserves are all vital things for developing an undefeated mind.

Building an undefeated mind takes time. However, it doesn't always require huge efforts. You can start practicing it right now by developing simple habits, pushing yourself in small everyday tasks, increasing your confidence, shifting your attitude, challenging yourself, actively doing what you've been tempted to avoid, sticking to a consistent behavior pattern and staying motivated.

Having said that, you should also learn to identify the pursuits that are not going to be worthy of your time and effort. You may be extremely capable, resilient, mentally strong and determined. However, you still won't be able to affect every single element that could influence your life. You have to be pragmatic and wise enough to realize that there's only so much you can have control over. Some factors are just beyond your control. Focus your energy away from those elements and towards aspects you can control.

Mental strength is much like muscle strength. It has its limitations. You may not be able to apply it for every task. Concentrate your efforts on what you can do and leave aside what you can't. For instance, you are immensely concerned about global warming negatively impacting the environment for our future generations. Here are things you can do – vote, offer constructive suggestions at the community/national level to curb carbon emissions, buy from eco-friendly brands, recycle and decrease your personal carbon footprint. This is what you can do even if you can't make everyone else adopt these lifestyle changes.

Do not complicate the concept of an undefeated mind by trying to keep going for something which isn't beneficial to you or your overall goal. It has to be directed towards things you need and want in life, and not just about everything that comes your way. Save your undefeated mind for things that matter, rather than spending it on every futile pursuit or distraction.

Developing mental strength is not an overnight process. It's not magic like "Voila, I am mentally tough today!" It takes consistent effort, unending reserves of patience and conscious changes in attitude. Some things in life will invariably be larger than us, but an undefeated mind will be your arsenal when it comes to adapting to the blows rather than succumbing to them. Once you master the ability to develop reasonable expectations, control your emotions, strengthen your motivation and build the patience to carry things through until the end, you will be geared to handle life with ease.

We are often tempted to lean towards instant gratification or saying yes to the easy way out. However, great achievements in life never come easy. It takes sweat and blood, patience and an iron will to manifest our dreams. All this is an undefeated mind. It is all about delaying gratification by keeping your vision firmly focused on the long-term goal. It is about persevering in the face of an overpowering feeling to throw it all up for instant relief. Now that we understand the concept of an undefeated mind, let us delve deeper into 10 power-packed strategies that will help us achieve our goals, full-throttle.

Chapter 2: Develop Emotional Stability

Want to achieve immense success in life? Ensure you are able to manage your emotions well because your performance in every life sphere heavily relies on your ability to effectively control your emotions. Many people fail to understand that our emotions are a double edged sword which can serve as both powerful motivators and unfortunate barriers. Our emotions have the power to get the better of us and can turn out to be a liability in our goal achievement process.

Whether you are an entrepreneur, a student or a sportsperson, emotional instability can inhibit your ability to stay focused and consistent in your actions during tough situations. Cynical thoughts, negativity and emotional fluctuations can be detrimental to your goal achievement. It will eventually take its toll and extract precious energy that could be used more productively.

Emotional stability allows us to get a firm grasp over our emotions and manage them effectively to deal with life's trials. When we are able to handle ourselves well under pressure without succumbing to acute emotional responses, we develop a formidable strength that helps us overcome our stumbling roadblocks. Treat your mind as the steering wheel of a car and realize that you are in the driver's seat. You can decide how you want to feel. You, not someone else, are responsible for how you feel. This is key number one for developing a greater undefeated mind.

Problems or Challenges?

Do you treat tough situations in life as problems or as challenges? It is easy to indulge in a pity party when life knocks you down. However, it's mighty tough to treat it as another occurrence beyond your control and overcome it by taking the required action. Take complete introspective stock of your emotions to boost your emotional stability. Are you quickly affected by the things that happen around you? Do you find yourself going nuts when things don't go according to plan? Do you get affected by small things enough to overlook the bigger picture?

Refrain From Whining

Start developing greater emotional stability by staying away from the urge to whine about things that are beyond your control, and instead, start to consciously focus on solutions that are within it. We often whine about a situation so excessively that we lose sight of the things we have going for us. This distracts us from our goals only to focus on things that keep us from achieving them. An undefeated mind is having the power to endure, sustain and manage our emotions by modifying our thinking.

Compartmentalize Emotions

One of the best ways to boost your emotional stability and subsequently acquire an undefeated mind is to be an "emotion compartmentalizing maven". These people are champs at saving one aspect of their life from spilling into another. They can efficiently keep away areas that are stressful from the productive ones. Say, for instance, an emotionally stable athlete playing a crucial qualifier game will not let their performance be hindered by a tumultuous personal relationship. He/she will know how to demarcate the two aspects of life to stop one from impacting the other.

To develop mental toughness, you need to realize that having one part of your life deeply affected doesn't translate into your entire life being affected. Identify the stress inducers and refrain from carrying them into more productive life pursuits. To isolate stress, you need to identify where it's originating.

Realign Memories

Countless studies on memory conspicuously point to a single premise – memories can be altered each time we mentally go through them. It simply means you can change how you remember what you remember each time you recall it. Say you were crazily in love with a person and had wonderful memories of the time you were involved with him/her. One day, your relationship goes kaput. Now, when you think of him/her, you realize how he/she was such a depressive, sad and mentally unstable individual in several situations. You keep thinking of them as a lonely and negative, which eventually wipes your original positive memory of the good times you both shared and replaces it by more negative instances of your togetherness.

When we shift or re-align our memories, we facilitate more positive or negative feelings to direct our actions. You can simply affect the way you feel and act by consciously reframing your memory from being not so pleasant to being pleasant. It won't be the easiest thing to do, particularly if you've survived rather traumatic situations, but it will help you achieve greater emotional stability in the long run and ultimately develop an enviable mental resilience.

Surround Yourself With Emotionally Stable Folks

Being around emotionally toxic people will wrap you up in greater anxiety. You may not even realize you are being negative because it has become a deeply ingrained part of you. People who are emotionally unstable or who have regular mood swings can deeply impact your own feelings and attitude. Stick to people who are "drama-less", emotionally stable and don't mentally drain you. Learn what emotionally stable folks do differently and model your behavior on similar patterns. When you surround yourself with emotionally stable and positive people, you learn to cope better when things don't go your way.

Chapter 3: Positive Thinking is the Key

Positive thinking makes it simpler for you to think rationally and curb all those unnecessary negative thoughts that crop up periodically to keep you away from your fundamental goals. It takes some work to consistently get into a positive framework. However, once you master the art of shifting your perspective, it becomes more like second nature. You will find yourself thinking positively almost involuntarily, which will in turn manifest into more positive and constructive actions.

J.K. Rowling, the creator of the phenomenal Harry Potter series, had just been divorced and was barely making ends meet as a single mother on government aid. She also had to cope with the death of her mother who had passed away after a prolonged illness. This was just three years prior to the first Harry Potter book hitting the market. Rowling couldn't afford a computer or the cost of photocopying a novel of about 90,000 words. She had to manually type every version to send to various publishers, only to be rejected multiple times. A fairly unknown London-based publisher decided to give it another chance when the CEO's little daughter loved the story.

Despite all the challenges in her life, Rowling found it in her to stay positive and focus on creating an alternate realm of fantasy to make her readers happy. Rather than being bogged down by the sheer negativity surrounding her life, she stayed hopeful and kept tweaking her creative work until it was accepted to be published. She displayed a strong sense of positivity in the face of adversity. It was her positivity and undefeated mind that has today made her one of the world's richest and most loved authors. She could have easily been overcome by the negativity of the situation when she barely had enough to feed her baby. However, she let her imagination and positivity get the better of her in order to stay productive.

Rowling focused on creation and constructive energy rather than destruction. How many of us would display the same sense of determination in a similar situation? No wonder we aren't rolling in millions like her. When you are ready to pay the price life demands by being mentally tough in the face of adverse situations, the rewards will be equally magnificent.

Positive thinking pulls you from the realm of impossible . Don't we all shudder at the thought of what might have happened had Rowling been bogged down by those multiple rejections and simply stopped approaching publishers? Isn't that something most of us would have done? Simply focused on the impossible rather than shifting out thoughts into what could be even remotely possible. Winners find reasons; losers simply have a bunch of excuses.

Positive thinking keeps us afloat in the most daunting of circumstances. It helps build our undefeated mind by helping us look at the larger picture without being overwhelmed by temporary challenges. You learn to cling on to reasons when doing something rather than chasing escape routes for not doing something.

Dive into each task by thinking you will succeed, no matter what. This isn't simply egoistic or overly optimistic thinking. It is ensuring that your mind will be focused enough on productivity and will not be brought down by unproductive thoughts. Realize that support, motivation and strength have to come from within first in order to be mentally tough.

Visualization can facilitate positive thinking brilliantly. Try shutting your eyes and "mentally watching" yourself emerge victorious in a task even before you actually perform it. Imagine yourself succeeding in the task. Internalize all the feelings you will feel when you've successfully accomplished it. Regularly picture yourself successfully completing your tasks. When you do this, you activate the power of your subconscious mind in driving your actions. The subconscious mind won't be able to distinguish between the real and the imagined. It believes everything that enters its realm as real, thus channeling your actions in a particular direction.

Once you internalize feelings of victory in a game by constantly playing it in your mind, you invariably lead your subconscious to believe it, which in turn influences your actions to create it. Thus positive thinking is not merely a trendy life coaching catch phrase. It is a solid concept that can completely transform your life if you learn to harness its power.

When you throw positivity and positive thoughts into your subconscious realm, you are laying the foundation for instinctively positive actions that will take you a step closer to your goal. These positive thoughts and actions will be your ammunition in the face of challenges that distract you from your goal. Positivity will help you sustain through tough situations by focusing on what you can do rather than what you can't. It keeps your vision firmly focused on the bigger picture.

Try and keep repeating positive affirmations loudly to yourself for to enhance your mind's sense of positivity. This can be anything from "I will emerge victorious" to "I will perform xyz task to the best of my ability." These positive statements will lead your mind to truly believe it, and keep you going through trying times.

Chapter 4:Build Self-Confidence

The only constant things about our ever-changing life are the hurdles. We are all facing and dealing with some overwhelming challenge or another, from relationship issues to health woes to money problems. However, there's one thing winners do differently from losers. They do not keep others at the helm of their life and let them influence their emotions, drive their life's decisions, dictate their sense of self-worth and gain validation.

When you realize that no one but you can stop yourself from achieving what you want, you are in the driver's seat of your life, all buckled up for success! When you pass the reins of your life to others or depend on them for a sense of validation, you are far from being mentally tough. You are passing the keys of your feelings and actions into someone else's hands.

When you feel wonderful about yourself, there are few things you will believe you can't do and that will reflect in your performance. The sky will truly be the limit for you, as clichéd as it may sound. There will be a lesser tendency to fear opponents and external circumstances, for your shinning confidence light will be emitting from within. The confidence will reveal itself in everything, from your body language to your words to how you conduct yourself under tough circumstances. It's like you completely eliminate the apprehensions of losing and absolutely believe in your chances of emerging victorious.

International television superstar Oprah Winfrey's life was everything you pray every day your life shouldn't be. She grew up as a victim of racism, poverty and sexual abuse. Not just that, even as a celebrity, she faced body shaming, intrusive queries about her sexual orientation, and more. However, it far from shaped her opinion of who she was. The childhood and current tribulations did not color her reality of herself. It made her shine in an even more luminous light that radiated from within. Before the world believed in her, she believed in herself. She believed steadfastly in her ability to connect with people and understand their deepest emotions. When you see her in public today, the lady is a picture of poise and confidence. Nothing shakes her. From her eloquence with words to her ability to empathize with people to her self-assured body language - everything radiates self-confidence.

The best part of self-confidence is that it can be learned and built upon. It also requires regular work and maintenance efforts to sustain our confidence level. You may have to continuously evaluate yourself and make several adjustments along the way. Self-confidence is one of the realest ways to achieve both personal and professional goals. It comes from a belief that you know exactly what you are doing and what you are after strongly enough that very few obstacles can come in its way. Your self-confidence also inspires other people's belief in your abilities.

According to basketball sports psychology research, confidence is a crucial mental factor that differentiates successful and disappointing performances in several sports settings. Self-confidence comes with a firm belief that you can convert your biggest chance of failure into the biggest opportunity to emerge victorious. It comes with a clear belief, focused efforts and the ability to be unaffected by popular opinion or perception.

Self-confidence is realizing that success stems from failure. Absolute self-confidence is an unflinching belief in one's ability to give a remarkably good performance when it's required. It is the capacity to rise above external circumstances and pressure. It is primarily a relationship individuals develop with themselves. Making a firm decision to love oneself and believe in one's ability is one of the most surefire ways to build an emotional energy reserve required for continuous success.

Self confidence can be consciously developed by maintaining an encouraging support network, getting rid of negativity reminders, identifying your core skills, taking pride in the smallest achievements, being comfortable in your skin, being more self-accepting of your strengths and weaknesses, refraining from comparing yourself with others, learning to deal with your insecurities and admirably bouncing back from mistakes. Avoid being constantly bogged down by the perfection syndrome, and set realistic expectations for yourself. Be patient with yourself. Unlike what self-help gurus will have you believe, confidence is not a tonic that can be faked or instantly acquired. You have to help yourself earn it through consistency and efforts.

Self-confidence originates from knowing yourself and having a firm grasp on knowledge or skills related to your area of action. In the battle field, the general who wins is the one who knows everything about his enemy. When you make excellence or knowledge your strongest virtue, confidence will invariably follow. Bruce Lee famously said, "I fear not the man who has practiced 10,000 kicks once, but I fear the man who has practiced one kick 10,000 times."

Get to know yourself, identify your core strengths, start tuning into your mind, learn to cope with your negative thoughts and replace them with positive efforts. Think about your limitations. Are they real, imagined or conditioned limitations? Digging deep inside yourself will let you develop greater confidence.

Chapter 5: Learn To Delay Gratification

Well, we've discussed earlier how failure can actually be a beneficial stepping stone for your success. It can also be viewed as postponed gratification rather than simply failure. Being able to get a firm grip over your desire for immediate gratification can put you on the highway for an undefeated mind.

We are often tempted to say yes to the easy way out. It is a human tendency to escape whatever takes more effort and delays results. We want everything to happen instantly. Being able to say a vehement no to the easy way out and keep your focus on the long term vision allows you to develop an infallible undefeated mind. This requires you to stop dwelling on mistakes and learn from them, while moving on quickly. Gratification may be delayed, but that shouldn't take your concentration away from the larger goal.

Great things aren't always easy to do, and the ones that are easy are often not worth doing. When you are after a bigger accomplishment that's harder to achieve, the efforts and rewards will both be higher. The rewards will be worth it when you achieve what you were after. Are you willing to pay the price by sacrificing momentary pleasures for a greater goal?

Most achievers have perfected the art of not giving in to the impulse of short term pleasures for long term success. You need to sweat it out there, work intensely hard, be patient and focus on the bigger picture. There has to be a realization that things may sometimes not go your way. It takes patience, effort and time to accomplish challenging goals.

Real sports champions are certainly not created overnight. There is rigorous training, stamina building, restrained eating, strategy planning, muscle workouts, speed-increasing field practices and much more that goes into the creation of a sports star. We all admire their wealth, ludicrously high endorsement fees, sprawling homes and fancy lifestyles, giving little thought about the hard-work and delayed gratification that has gone into it. They might have been tempted to give up several times.

The pain during core strength training, the inability to eat whatever they want to, the desire to sleep a little extra instead of getting up for an intensive field practice session may have caused them inconvenience. However, their ability to look beyond it is what distinguishes them from the average folks who quickly surrender in the face of discomfort.

There may have been so many instances when they had simply wanted to quit the field due to pain and disappointment. However, they were able to make these tiny sacrifices for the bigger rewards. They were able to do what a majority of us find extremely challenging, because of our need for immediate returns. Our sporting heroes were able to keep themselves firmly fixated on their larger goals without worrying about temporary setbacks.

Working out in a gym is a great example of everything we need to follow in our life to give up temporary pleasures for long term success. Discipline, perseverance, determination and toughness are the lessons we can carry over into other aspects of our life as well. Think about anything from writing a book to being an artist – these are the exact qualifies you need in the "life's gym". An undefeated mind is as much about refusing yourself things that will hamper your long-term success as it is about persevering. Again, it's about grit.

Basketball superstar Michael Jordon has often been referred to as one of the world's best basketball players ever. However, the gifted athlete unfailingly credits his success to his innumerable failures because, according to him, they only pushed him to try harder. Rather than seeking immediate gratification (in the form of success) or giving up in the glaring face of failure, he kept going without getting discouraged. When he was young, he was seen as possessing mediocre game skills and wasn't taken too seriously. The man did something we would never dream of – Jordan counted his failures (300 lost games to be precise). He missed the game winning shot a whopping 26 times. Most people would've thought that maybe they weren't cut out for the game.

However, Michael Jordan had a different approach. For him, failure was merely a recipe for long term success. In his own words, "I know that fear is an obstacle for some people, but for me it is just an illusion. Failure always makes me try harder on the next opportunity." Brilliant.

Why is there just one Michael Jordon or one Lebron James when there are thousands of basketball players all over the world? What is the one trait that sets them apart from the average Joes? Why are they raking in millions while others are finding it tough to make ends meet? Because they made a decision to never quit despite the in-your-face failures, and because they delayed immediate gratification for the bigger goal.

Chapter 6: Be Courageous

Walt Disney famously said, "All our dreams can come true, if we have the courage to pursue them." The fear of failure can do you more harm than failure itself. You cannot win without believing in your goals and having the courage to actively pursue them. You have to be brave enough to take risks, change your strategy, alter your game plan and adjust to new changes in order to succeed.

You have to completely eliminate the fear of failure and be daring enough to chase your goals. Ever wondered why we always say, he/she has guts to do it when we refer to someone fearless? Because, according to several spiritual disciplines, the power center of a human being is housed in their gut. This simply symbolizes that all the power to accomplish a goal is tied to our gut, or having a lot of guts (courage).

Courage separates the winners from the also-rans. It suppresses the fear of failure and replaces it with a more formidable feeling of just going out there and giving it your best. Courage can be manifested in any form from standing up for what you truly believe in to remaining composed in the face of intense competition to tackling your insecurities to maintaining dignity in defeat. Fearlessness can make you a world-class athlete in the trial blazing race of life.

Courage is one of the most vital cornerstones of an undefeated mind. Contrary to popular belief, it isn't simply lack of fear. Courage can be inspired by fear as well. There has to be a fearful element to make you feel the courage. There has to be a stimulus of fear, which will then make you feel above it. The brave and the coward both experience fear. However, the brave knows how to rise above the fear while the coward grapples with it. The coward's immediate response is to get away from the discomfort, while the courageous one goes on and does whatever he/she is afraid of doing, irrespective of the fear.

When he was a young lad of 14, actor Jim Carrey's dad was rendered jobless and the entire family witnessed rough times. They lived in a VW van on a distant relative's lawn premises. Young Carrey took up an eight hours a day job in a factory to help the family survive. At the age of 15, he performed his stand up comedy act onstage for the very first time, which totally bombed. At 16, he was again heckled after a routine comic performance at a night club in LA. He drove to Mulholland Drive that night and wrote himself the now famous check for $10,000,000 with "Acting Services Rendered" clearly mentioned on it. The check bore the date of Thanksgiving 1995. He carried it in his wallet all the time while relentlessly pursing acting jobs. Just before the date of his check, he got his paycheck for Dumb and Dumber, and the rest, as they say, is history.

A lot of people in a similar situation might have been frightened by the prospect of putting everything at stake to pursue their talent. In dire circumstances, and in the face of constant criticism, people would have been tempted to simply quit and take up a regular job. Carrey was hooted away from his first performance (and many after that). Just imagine the consequences of him quitting at that time or taking up another job believing he would eventually fail as a comedian.

If a few heckles could have scared him away from his goal, we wouldn't have been able to enjoy his laugh a riot comedies and he wouldn't be the revered performer he is today. This is courage. The belief to write yourself a check of $10,000,000 and believing in it, shortly after you've been booed away from a performance can only be the result of a courageous mind that isn't afraid to dream and that believes in the power of those dreams enough to manifest them.

Helen Keller is another shining example of courage. Born perfectly healthy, she became blind and deaf due to an unidentified illness at the tender age of 19 months. She could have spent an entire lifetime cursing her bad fortune and fearful circumstances. However, she chose to rise above the fear and became the first visually and hearing impaired person to receive a Bachelor of Arts degree in 1900.

Keller later went on to become an internally renowned crusader for the welfare of the people with disabilities. What was it in her that made her stand apart from the rest? It was her fearlessness even in the face of the most turbulent setbacks. Rather than wallowing in self-pity and being afraid to venture into the world around her due to her disabilities, she chose to make those disabilities a part of her strength and worked relentlessly for the betterment of those like her. Keller converted what was considered a disability into a formidable source through which others could draw inspiration.

Chapter 7: Bounce Back When Life Knocks You Down

Legend has it that Thomas Edison created several thousand prototypes of the light bulb before he actually got it all figured out. The prolific inventor of over 1,000 patents failed almost every day at his Menlo Park lab. Game changers are excellent in rebounding from mistakes, failures and disappointments to get back head-on into their game. They immediately make the changes wherever required. They are resolute about making things better rather than simply giving up.

Despite wrestling with failure almost all through his professional life, Edison never let failure get the better of his ingenuity. The tens of thousands of failed inventions (yes, that much) were merely an indication of how not to do something for him, which pointed him to the direction of what actually worked. Edison's resilience gave us some of the most path-breaking 20th century inventions that made our lives simpler.

Can you imagine what the world around us would be like if he had simply decided to give up after the initial fails? Do you have that kind of resilience to pursue your goals? Or do you simply let a few failures throw you off the dream track? Do you realize what you could accomplish if only you could maintain the strength to refrain from giving up?

Resilience is our ability to bounce back when things don't go according to plan. While these seemingly unfortunate blows overwhelm the majority of people, resilient people quickly adapt to the situation to emerge even more successful. They don't wallow under their failures, but simply learn from them and move on.

Resilient folks do not perceive themselves as unfortunate victims of circumstances. Rather, their time and efforts are concentrated on elements they can control. These people seldom worry about what opinion others hold of them, and they maintain wholesome relationships without succumbing to peer pressure. They have very solid goals and an even more powerful desire to achieve them.

Resilience arises from positively envisioning your future. There is a more positive overall outlook that helps them get back into the game of life despite several unsuccessful moves. Developing a resilient mindset makes us immune to stress, adversity, failure and circumstances beyond our control. Rather than becoming reactive victims, we become proactive warriors and write our own destiny.

People who are resilient see the consequences of unfortunate events as temporary setbacks and not permanent failure. For example, they are more likely to say "My professor didn't like this particular research project of mine" over "my professor hated my work." They don't let setbacks in one particular area affect their entire life. They will say they aren't good at something rather than that they are bad at everything they do.

Resilient individuals spend their time and effort engaged in activities they can control. Since their efforts are directed where they can have maximum impact, these people feel more confident, positive and empowered. They don't expend their energies on uncontrollable elements or waste time feeling helpless, victimized and powerless. The manner in which we perceive our failures is extremely crucial to developing an undefeated mind. The bitter truth is, we all fail, some time or the other. The only people who don't fail are the ones who never try and live a shuttered life. Failure is a sign you are trying and taking risks. A meager existence that is devoid of failure is not something you want, is it?

Here are some Tips to Develop Greater Resilience

Resilience can be developed by learning to manage stress through exercise and sleeping well. When you care for your mental and physical well being, you are able to efficiently cope with life's challenges.

Practicing thoughtful awareness is another brilliant way to fine-tune your resilience. Folks that do this do not let negativity destroy their efforts but focus on positive thinking. When things go wrong, pay close attention to the dialogue in your head. Do you make more sweeping statements that are all pervasive and permanent? If the answer is yes, start by amending these thoughts into thoughts that are temporary and only related to the current pursuit and not your overall life.

Practice complete cognitive restructuring to alter your thinking about negative events and circumstance beyond your control.

Understand that failures can be treated as learning opportunities for growth. Every mistake or so-called failure comes with a hidden opportunity to help you learn an important lesson. Learn to absorb the lesson behind every failure. Heard of post-traumatic growth? Well, yes, what doesn't kill you indeed makes you stronger.

You cannot choose everything that happens to you, but you can very well choose your response. We have a powerful choice in responding to things that happen to us. We can either get all worked up about unfortunate events or situations or we can choose to stay composed and work our way through it to find a reasonable solution. Always remember - even if nothing is up to you, your reaction is.

Always maintain perspective. Resilient folks correctly realize that the impact of a crisis or event, though currently overwhelming, may not have a long-term bearing.

They stay away from blowing things out of proportion and they always remember to maintain perspective.

Make sure your goals are smart, realistic and achievable. Setting goals that are in sync with your value system and learning from every experience is vital for developing resilience.

Developing strong interpersonal relationships will ensure that you have a powerful support system to lean on. The more real friends and solid work connections you build, the easier it will be for you to bounce back with the help of their support and encouragement.

Staying flexible is the key to boosting your resilience and acquiring an undefeated mind. Resilient folks recognize that even the most meticulously framed plans can go awry and are always ready to adapt, amend or scrap their plans in accordance with the circumstances thrown their way.

Chapter 8: Embrace Challenges

Mentally tough individuals thrive in shifting and challenging situations. They flourish in an environment that is rapidly changing or that offers them brand new opportunities for growth and development. People who are constantly embracing challenges develop the ability to be resourceful and think out of the box, which consequently makes them mentally tougher. They develop a keen knack for creativity, accepting risks and exploring innovative approaches. All this is geared towards accomplishing positive outcomes, which aren't deterred by a few setbacks.

Mentally tough people realize that difficulties, uncertainties and new opportunities are all a part of life, and wholeheartedly pursue challenges, for they know that it brings out the best in them. They aren't afraid to take risks because they understand that the higher risks have the potential to bring higher gains.

Steve Jobs and Steve Wozniak launched Apple when Jobs was a 20-year old. Their decade long hard-work resulted in Apple growing from a "garage company" into a staggering $2 billion firm with more than 4000 employees on its payroll. In 1983, Pepsi's John Sculley was hired to be the new Apple CEO. Jobs and Sculley had major management0-related differences, which eventually forced Jobs to resign from his own firm.

According to Jobs, it turned out to be a huge blessing in disguise. He was a creative newcomer again rather than a complacent successful entrepreneur. In Jobs' own words, "It freed me to enter one of the most creative periods of my life." See what he did there? He turned a seemingly challenging situation on its head by converting it into one of the most productive and gratifying years of his life. Far from seeing the monumental change of being thrown out of his own company as a disaster, Jobs consciously worked towards making it a gratifying experience.

Few of us have the ability to spot the hidden opportunity in a tragedy or challenge. We simply do not realize that challenges can indeed be blessings in disguise. Have you found yourself unfairly chucked out of a job only to be able to find a more fulfilling and rewarding career opportunity? Or missed an opportunity only to be awarded an even bigger one? When you learn to embrace challenges and seize them as brilliant chances to prove your worth, you will be displaying a remarkable undefeated mind.

Challenges are a huge source of our personal development and growth. Can you even imagine a completely challenge-free life where everything is wonderful forever? How long do you think you would enjoy such a life? Challenges build self-confidence. When you overcome an intensely challenging situation, your belief in yourself soars. We consider something to be a huge challenge when it impacts a crucial aspect of our life. Solving a huge challenge automatically adds to our confidence level.

Martin Luther King Jr. said "The ultimate measure of a man is not where he stands in moments of comfort and convenience, but where he stands at in times of challenge and controversy." Pick up the biography of any illustrious historic leader and you will notice, they have rarely had a smooth sailing life. Their lives have been checkered with mishaps, uncertainties and adverse events. There have been plenty of bumps along their life paths, which were handled with remarkable fortitude. This toughness is what led them to achieve the success and following they did. Remember, even a diamond has to withstand years of intense pressure for it to convert from an ordinary coal into an extraordinarily sparkling diamond.

Challenges offer you a deep sense of accountability. They offer you guidance, and most importantly, take you a step closer to your goal (even if you may not realize it immediately). Challenge yourself to do what seems impossible. It can be anything from a 30-day sobriety challenge (which will eventually get you out of the habit of excessive alcohol consumption if you're committed to achieving it) to getting a degree. The seemingly impossible tasks you give yourself need not be huge challenges, they can start with simplistic every day things like cutting down on your daily sugar intake or walking more.

Successfully fulfilling these goals can also award you with a feeling of immense accomplishment, which slowly builds up your resolve, and convinces you of your capacity to achieve just about anything you want. This, in turn, increases your mental strength.

Chapter 9: Develop Flexibility

Mental strength relies heavily on how flexible you are in your thinking and approach. Do you always look for new ways to resolve challenging situations? Do you possess the knack for absorbing uncertainties and remaining supple in the face of adversities? Do you have the ability to stay non-defensive and retain humor even in tough situations? Flexibility is needed in all spheres of life to re-educate yourself and realign the ideas you hold with the realities of the world around you. Coaches may have to immediately think of a new way to get the ball down the playing field after a quarterback faces a broken play. Adaptability, flexibility and quick decision making are strong indicators of an undefeated mind.

Flexibility by no means translates into constantly trying to alter your behavior patterns to suit your circumstances or other people around you. It simply means to focus on those activities or situations where you can choose to show a little less rigidity for the overall good.

Flexibility is not to be applied to areas like ethics, core value or principles. It talks more about adapting and adjusting to newer ways of doing things and re-shifting your ideas or perspective for the bigger picture. For instance, you may have a more authoritative management style which has worked with the older employees but the newer employees may respond more effectively to a democratic management style. Thus, for the overall benefit of the organization and to boost productivity and profits, you may have to adopt a more democratic functioning style.

Even the best chalked out plans in life can go awry, and those who do not possess the ability to deal with disruptions by being flexible may subject themselves to a lot of stress. Learning to relax by changing your approach will allow you to live a more enjoyable and varied life.

Here are Some Power-packed Ways to Boost your Mental Stability

Always break down your goals into smaller tasks and give priority to the tasks that have the maximum impact on the overall goal. This gives you the flexibility to adopt different approaches when fulfilling the smaller tasks to show you that the end result can be achieved even by doing things slightly differently.

Always try to handle criticism in a constructive manner. If it is based on sound knowledge, you may be required to alter your thinking or approach from the other person's point of view. This will help not just your growth and development, but also your ability to quickly adapt to new approaches.

Try to avoid stressing or fussing over things that are beyond your control. Some things are just beyond your circle of influence and you can do nothing about them. Focus on things that are actually within your realm of control, and wield power over them.

In your constant quest to be perfect, also make an effort to focus on how you treat others by adapting or staying flexible to their feelings.

At work, have belief in your colleague's abilities and delegate appropriate tasks to them by displaying faith and respect. In the event of their inability to complete the task, offer guidance rather than taking the task upon yourself. This will give you the ability to be a little more flexible where other work styles and ideas are concerned. Approach everything, from your personal life to work, with a strong desire to improve.

Give others a chance to be themselves and appreciate them for who they are, rather than trying to alter their individuality. This will allow you to have more meaningful and fulfilling interpersonal relationships.

Always be ready to try out new skills, learn from new tasks and to be a part of different teams.

Try rewarding yourself for flexibility in place of perfection. Rather than applauding yourself for doing something perfectly, try appreciating the fact that you did something differently for a change.

Learn from mistakes. Identify what you could have done differently, absorb it and quickly move on by internalizing the lesson. If you keep doing the same thing despite the glaring negative outcomes, it may affect your efficiency and overall well-being. You have to learn to adapt and do things differently to witness stellar results!

Train yourself to be a little more flexible by challenging behavior patterns and routines that can be slightly tweaked. For example, if you do your laundry on any particular day of the week, try shifting the chore to another day or take a different route on your way to work each morning. Learn to consciously break the mould by doing things differently.

Chapter 10: Manage Stress Effectively

Learning to effectively manage stress can be the foundation for developing greater mental strength. When you use a variety of ways to deal with your stress, you not only witness its benefits in the form of good health, emotional stability and better performance, but also boost your capacity for dealing with adverse situations. This invariably ups your quotient of an undefeated mind.

In addition to physical disorders, stress also contributes to several psychological and mental disorders. It can manifest itself in the form of phobias, depression, anxiety and other emotional dysfunctions. Psychological stress makes it challenging for us to focus, make logical decisions and remember details. It can also cause greater irritability, extreme emotions (such as anger and insecurity) and deep interpersonal relationship issues. When we are bogged down by the physical and mental effects of stress, staying mentally tough becomes a huge challenge.

Effective stress management techniques allow us to cope with all the stress-inducing external factors that can hinder our development. It helps us rise above the situation to overcome difficult scenarios without getting bogged down by them or giving in. There can be several stress-inducing factors that are completely outside your control. However, how you deal with them is up to you. When you learn to efficiently deal with your stress, you give yourself the power to stay unaffected in the most daunting of situations.

All the top performers have well-tuned strategies for coping with stressful situations. They ensure that whatever happens in their environment seldom affects them, and even if they do experience some amount of stress – it is not prolonged. There are some tried and tested ways through which you can better manage your stress, stay unaffected by things you cannot control and boost your overall productivity, which in turn significantly impact your undefeated mind.

Here are Some Powerful Stress Management Tips

Commit to about 10-20 minutes of daily mediation. It can be as simple as deep breathing or practicing mindfulness.

Engaging in a regular and fun-filled exercise routine such as swimming, dance, yoga, aerobics and cycling also reduces stress and increases your overall well-being. Moderate physical activity leads to release of the stress busting endorphin hormones, which in turn keeps you in a more positive frame of mind. Exercising regularly boosts your confidence and decreases symptoms related to depression, which allows you to show greater strength and control in the face of adversity.

Eat healthy by focusing more on nutrition and less on high sugar comfort foods. Consume a diet comprising of fresh veggies and fruits, lean protein and nutritious whole grains.

Get enough sleep and avoid relying on alcohol, drugs, nicotine, caffeine and other addictive elements to combat stress. It will only add to your woes.

Learn to assertively say no to unproductive things that drain your energy. Be very clear about establishing your limits and don't fall into the trap of trying to please everyone.

Prayers are a brilliant channel for helping you manage stress. It can be a prayer addressed to any force such as God, nature, the universe or anything that drives you. Research has consistently pointed to the fact that people who pray (religiously or spiritually) are much calmer than people who do not.

Grow a garden if you can. Tending to plants helps you commune beautifully with nature, a wonderful and proven stress reliever. Even if you cannot have a full-fledged garden, nurture a houseplant. Plants represent growth, prosperity and the circle of life –a nice reminder of the philosophy that the stressful situation shall pass.

People's body language can add to their stress. When people are extremely stressed, they walk like they are carrying the entire world's difficulties on their back. Slumping inhibits breathing and reduces the supply of oxygen and blood to the brain, which adds to the body's muscle tension. This further amplifies feelings of helplessness, anxiety and panic. Straighten up your spine and walk like you own the world.

Talking to a family member or close friend you can trust is a great way to unburden yourself. Just having a loved one listen to you without interrupting you can be therapeutic. This will not just reduce your stress but also put into a more positive mindset for overcoming the obstacles in your life.

Write about it. Writing offers you a unique perspective that you may not have otherwise considered. Make a list of all the things that are completely in your control and things that are not. Now focus on what you can control and stop stressing over things you cannot.

Chapter 11: Practice Greater Self-Awareness

Self-awareness is the threshold of personal growth, change and development. It is virtually impossible to be a great athlete, for instance, if you aren't aware of your core strengths and weaknesses. An undefeated mind comes when you have a high enough understanding of yourself to prepare for any adverse situation. When you possess greater self-awareness, you learn to trust your ability, display stronger mental skills and optimize your performance. The better you assess yourself in all spheres of life, and the more you absorb from each undertaking, the higher your undefeated mind will soar.

An undefeated mind is the ability to withstand challenging events or circumstances in your life, while single-mindedly pursing your goals. You can only cope effectively with challenges when you are aware of the inner resources you can use to combat them. A warrior can hardly fight without being aware of his weapons and how he can use them in the best way. An athlete can hardly emerge victorious in an edge of the seat game without harnessing his/her most dominant skills and overcoming his/her weaknesses. A performer can never truly earn accolades until he/she learns to harness their gifts into a sparkling performance. Here's how you can boost your self-awareness.

Make Self-Reflection a Habit

Make self-reflection a regular habit by devoting some time of the day to reflect on the day's events. This practice lets you concentrate on things that matter, while letting go of things beyond your sphere of control. Rather than focusing on immediate goals, focus on overall life objectives. Self-reflection or mindfulness impacts your mental faculties and directs feelings of anxiety to ones of calmness and overall well-being. It helps you understand what really motivates you and what your core values are. It is like taking a stock inventory of your typical characteristics and traits.

Reflection can happen in any form, from keeping a journal to saying a prayer to practicing mindful meditation to taking a long walk. If you are able to center into yourself and focus your entire being on what really matters to you, you will develop a powerful sense of inner peace and well-being sooner or later.

Seek Genuine Feedback

We all possess some unique traits that aren't visible to us as subjective evaluators of our own personality. "Blind spots" are traits we have but are unable to view in ourselves. Does your opinion of yourself match others' opinions of you? Why is it that you don't see yourself like others do? You can tackle these blind spots by soliciting genuine feedback from well-meaning folks whom you can implicitly trust. Don't let unreasonable psychological triggers stop you from asking for wholesome feedback. Getting defensive will only hinder the process of getting to know yourself objectively.

Analyze Your Attitude

Attitude is often a result of expectations. Sometimes, our expectations are unrealistic and tinged by a heavy dose of fear or pessimism. For instance, your attitude on racism can say a lot about the type of person you are. Also, your attitude in this instance is not helpful in judging the people around you in a diverse society. This attitude is clearly something people often internalize from the world around them. Similarly, a lot of our negative attitudes about ourselves are limiting and in no way indicate our true potential. It may simply be a limiting perception that is created by your family and friends, which might have gone unchallenged with you. Knowingly or unknowingly, you may have been led to believe things about you which are not true.

Take Psychometric Tests

Psychometric tests, such as the Predictive Index and Myers-Briggs tests are a great way to create a data point for developing higher self-awareness. These tests have no specifically correct and incorrect answers. They are comprehensively designed to compel users to consider personality traits and characteristics that best describe them. Respondents are required to get into a sort of reflective mode to mull over the choices that come closest to their persona. There are choice questions that help respondents gain a deeper understand of their true fundamental traits – e.g. Are your actions primarily driven by results or passion? Would you describe yourself as more analytical or instinctive?

Look For Specific Behavior Patterns

Identify typical behavior patterns that manifest themselves in certain situations. Do you constantly find yourself blaming others for your shortcomings? Do you give others the ability to completely control your feelings and emotions? Do you find yourself giving in too easily to the demands of your loved ones? Pin down these specific characteristics and consciously work towards eliminating them with a change in behavior.

For instance, if you find yourself easily giving in to people, try to display more assertiveness by firmly saying no when you aren't up for a task. Get out of habits and behavior patterns that are energy suckers and focus on developing more productive traits that can help you stay mentally tough and achieve your goals in the long run. Make a list of your most compelling priorities, and work on eliminating behavior patterns that are not in sync with it. Identify your likes and dislikes and stay away from unproductive pursuits that consume your time and from doing things just because other people expect you to.

Conclusion

I hope this book was able to help you develop keen insights about the ways through which you can get closer to having an undefeated mind, and finally achieve the goals you've set your heart on.

Let's recap the 10 Keys for An undefeated mind We Have Discussed:

1. Develop emotional stability

2. Remember positive thinking is the key

3. Build self-confidence

4. Learn to delay gratification

5. Be bold and courageous

6. Bounce back when life knocks you down

7. Embrace challenges

8. Develop flexibility

9. Manage stress effectively *and* 10. Practice greater self-awareness

The next step is to make all the 10 keys of goal achievement a habit and consciously incorporate them into your everyday life, in order to transform yourself more fully.

Lastly, if you enjoyed reading this book; please take the time to share your insights and feedback by posting a review of Amazon. It'd be highly appreciated.

Made in the USA
Monee, IL
15 July 2022

99742242R00026